Woman
Reading
in Bath

Woman Reading in Bath

POEMS BY ANNE SZUMIGALSKI

Doubleday Canada Ltd.
Toronto, Ontario

Doubleday & Company, Inc.
Garden City, New York

1974

Some of these poems first appeared in the following publications:

"Videotape" first appeared in *The Canadian Forum* (1968).

"Granny Looks at the Stars" in *Other Voices* (1968) and in *Skylark*.

"Victim" in *Fiddlehead* and in FIFTEEN WINDS (Ryerson 1969).

"Ergot and After," "Visitors' Parking," "Early Sorrow," "The Meditation Look," "Ribgrass" all first appeared in *Skylark*.

"Biting the Hand" in *Wascana Review* (1967).

"Novella" in *Auricle* (1971).

"Letters from Home" and "Girl with a Basket" in FORTY WOMEN POETS OF CANADA (Ingluvin 1972).

"Elizabeth Renders," "Crabseeds," and "Night Sermons" in SASKATOON POETS 1971–72 (Mendel Gallery).

"Stefan Sequence," "Nettles," "What a Girl Has" in PRAIRIE (Mendel Gallery 1973).

"No Approach," "Untitled" in *Elfin Plot*.

"Where Are You Arthur Silverman?" and "A Celebration" in *Salt*.

Library of Congress Cataloging in Publication Data

Szumigalski, Anne, 1922–
  Woman reading in bath.

  Poems.
  I. Title.
PR6069.Z88W6   821'.9'14
ISBN: 0-385-02743-5 Trade
      0-385-07586-3 Paperback
Library of Congress Catalog Card Number 73–15478

WITH LOVE
TO MOLLY MADCAP AND THE MAJOR

Contents

III *Nettles*

I Crabseeds

Where Are You Arthur Silverman?

She told me how it was when I was born
how they took a long knife thin as a leaf
and slashed her up and down and tore
me waxed and silent out of her

"Why Mother why
was I suffocating in the slack flesh of your bowels?
was I stuck in the grip of your stony pelvis?
did I gasp?
did my mouth fill with slime?"

> *"Darling it was the nails of you so sharp*
> *you could have cut five-lane pathways with your feet*
> *It was the head of you so great*
> *You could have burst all my sexy bits*
> *and so they cut me up*
> *and you came out with a bloody head"*

taking my hand in hers to touch the scar
the ropy knotted scar
I felt on her dark belly that ladder thing
to climb up and kiss her smiling face
but *"no"* I said *"no no"*

I laced up my sandal thongs
and got into my dune car
and drove away from her over soft sand
for miles to see the Sphinx

I had to feel how granite meets the sand
and how the ocean touches the shore
I had to fly until my rocket broke
the ceiling of the universe (it was only
hoop paper and burst quite easily)
over my shoulder I shouted to my mother
"tomorrow when I come back be gone
be dead   be buried   be forgotten"

       "then who will take care of my dust" she whispered

now in the sullen center of the city
I think of her often   sometimes on seeing old
and austere nuns leaving their house in double file
and their speckly withered hands all woven about
with beads   click click they softly all together
the low musical quaver of their dear old voices
easing away the flesh from the pure calcium
of their most holy bones
              not so my mother with her untrained meat
body boundless   no doubt she leaps up still
distributing her folds less neatly than a manatee
or doesn't she sit somewhere offering to let you
feel her great scar for a dollar?

all haggy she sits in the road
and spits wetly on policemen's trousers
as they drag her sagging bulk towards the wagon

that grimy old whore
will she never keep quiet?

Come Sisters and wash her from sins and spittle
frock her in blue cotton and set her in the sun
on a scrubbed wooden chair
in the kitchen garden

and teach her how to knit graveclothes
for the innocent

Letters from Home

Is this the mountain where the ark rested?
Eyelid opened its shutters and out
Flew doves   They found me
I am in the desert looking up

When the walls split we fell into this trap
And we are stranded in the Bitter Lakes

Prow between boulders—keel hanging out
And mild white-shouldered girls lie
Folded in my bunk all through the heat
This one   that one sweating between the hinges
Of my limbs says *hand me the green striped*
Towel Harry says *part O part my hair*
Lying between us like rough bark

We are walking on decks as hot as sidewalks
Cement burns blister us between the toes
But I want peeled wood
I want rain in the hills
I want oak barrels
I want to see my mother in her cheap felt boats
Dancing on the gray snows of March

When the walls split we fell into this trap
And we are stranded in the Bitter Lakes

Early Sorrow

it happened in Saskatoon
where the sky is high and
the brass sun over the bridge
is shaking in the heat
and I am walking with the girl
with the oriental eyes

look how she leaves tracks
wild tacks in the dust of her footprints
her toenails need cutting and I say
"dear let me cut them" but
"they might bleed" she says

I wish my seed had settled in her
secret place but I cannot see myself
holding the child's hand
a child with blue slant eyes
red frizz top and feet that don't match?
and Oh hell why didn't I?

that was the day she came with me to the park
they all came and sat down elbow to elbow
in the long grass eating
out of each other's pockets
love love we sang quietly all together
crushing the weeds with wet sounds
blowing out smoke between our clenched teeth

but I watch my girl as she sets down
her small brown silky lotus bum
among the dandelions
darling cross your legs
so that ants won't crawl in that honey crack
I am to be bee and not that melancholy Spaniard
who beckons with stained fingers
he calls her away with fingers on the strings
and sound moves   it jumps and clicks
on the rings of his fingers

night it alone shall I?
shall I send on her few small folded panties
gold thongs of her broken sandals?
shall I send her a cheerful letter wherever she is
gone from one hand to the other
or still with the Spaniard's
stained fingernails breaking
the skin of those olive thighs

six cents for a stamp
I could have mailed myself through that slit
but no I am a hollow boy   hollow as a guitar
and without strings to tie my parcel

Crabseeds

A man I used to know
Has become my child
One day his mouth grew hard and small
Trying not to let me catch him smiling

From caress of finger
From breathy sticky kiss
He got nothing but a command
To sleep and sleep over
From day to day

Pips in an apple rattle
Like the hurt seeds of his mind
Under his low tread
The fruit breaks and opens
And shells out from sharp capsule
Its small brown stones

Bring me an old plate
And set it under the tree
I want to arrange the crabseeds
So as to resemble
Some kind of disorder

Victim

Ah the cliff edge—where so many murders are done
Can't you see the body among the boulders
Far down on the beach?
While seagulls scream they are filming
A frail girl in a thin nightgown
Prone on the distant rocks

Mr. B and I are walking hand in hand
Up the cliff path knowing
That under our feet
Disaster and drama are making a second-rate movie
Take no notice my darling Mr. B
Tell me a simple answer to the urgent question
Who am I?   Who are we?

Mr. B is a known madman   a suspected murderer
I think the cops are after him for being himself
For not sobbing
For not beating his breast
When he finds a victim on the beach
Bloody and wet in the tide
Was that my body we saw down there Mr. B
Twisted in seaweed   Who am I?   Who was I?

He picked me up on the beach

I am the tiny girl in the thin nightgown
That Mr. B carries in a seashell
In his trousers pocket among
The sticks of Dentyne gum and the spent flashbulbs
Oh I am glad I am dead and can't see
The dirty darkness in here

I was murdered last Thursday but even so
The heat of his groin
And all the fumbling that goes on there
Is disturbing my final rest

A Short Season

I want to walk
I want to walk on water
My feet will feel the swell
And I will sway from side to side
On the rocking waves
Of the Lake of the Woods
      When I reach shore I will dry my feet
      On a black beachtowel printed
      All over with green mermaids
      Sand will grit between my toes
      But my knees will be as dry as driftwood
      I will sing to myself as I walk
      Through cheering crowds to the deep woods
      Beyond the claptrap cottages

Once I am out of sight
My Dad the Promoter will drive up
In his old-fashioned megaphone truck

How you will weep
Your tears will drip into the lake
Salting the sweet water

O gladly gladly you will give your dollars
When he takes up the collection
Just as the purple sun goes down

      "A *most successful evening*"
      Says the Old Man counting
      Wads and wads under the dark trees

Damn right Dad   it's a good trick for gains
But hell on the feet

There are so many thorns in the sand

Woman Reading in Bath

I am swimming alone on the dark sea
When before me looms up the great stout chin of god
Floating on the black chops of the high tide
And his hands are clutching the slippery wet sides
The edges and the hems of his bungled universe

What's this curling murderously around my neck?
What's this strangling over the blue knots of my neck?
Wiry fingers of hair thick knuckle-bladders
It is a long curled lock from the godhead
Red as sargassum

When the eye is shut then shall the great globe dim
Like a popped bulb scattering flakes
Of slowly falling volcano glass round
The vast bulges of softly swimming belly
And does the great thumping creator's heart
Somehow sit inside and direct the traffic
Of sharks and seals and obedient shoals?
Lucky and cunning from the dark I watch
The huge mouthful of deified teeth from which
Squeaks out a puny cry meant to be a roar
Great heave of the chest but yet a breath
So small it hardly blows my hair about
As I tread water in the shallows
Under the square shadow of his shoulders
        He heaves up on stick legs like a fat bird
Crack crack the shanks have snapped
And down he flops on the shingles gasping and stranded

I—the Director—pick up the phone
Connecting me to the sky and the undersea silt
I say *"Birds come down from the clouds"*
I say *"Great crabs come up from the deep*
Chew on this mass—feed all your children
On it for a year"

Oh what a dry and brittle skeleton he makes
But on the last day a small bone hand shall creep
Out of the gray shore sand
And grasping a pebble throw it over my head
Into deep water

Who are you knocking at
my lionshead brass doorpiece?
are you a salesman got small samples
of face oil and polish?
got good fillers for the rosegarden?

No
I am a speaker
I speak for weak words
that have outdistanced the mind

Birdie Thomas leaning his head
against my doorpost to pray
I want to say—*stop*
you are weeping down the paint
you are spoiling my marigolds

come in do
into my wide house
haven't you got your hands
round the inside doorknob
haven't you got your fingers
in the warm already?

While we were inside and
the shag rug sprouting between our toes
came the flagmen from the interior
they came with their white masts and
nailed them down into the roof
above our heads
there were quite twenty standards
some provinces I never heard of yet

and all with their appropriate symbols
such as round midnight suns
and reddened fish in milky water

I wonder why Thomas
while you sleep no eagle
comes and perches on your masthead?
every flagpole should have its buzzard
or sinister peregrine
I know a man would say pigeons
but Birdie and I safe in the pillows
do not lend an ear

Here the little man is awakened to the sunny afternoon
Thomas in the shade of maples walking
on broken concrete between rows of pansies
opening his bag he brings out
clipboards full of yellow pages
sometimes the wind that whips at the flags
whips away the papers too
I find myself running on thorny ground
picking notes from the bushes

the door is the door to a garden
walled around with fieldstones
I grow what I can in this dry prairie air
my house has no doors
it has only arches through which
snow will blow and cake up the furniture
come winter—and shred the flags
and freeze the buds and the deadheads
making them all sag down together
behind the wire fences

Birdie's in the garden ranting
in his neatly zippered boots

a voice from a woolly hood
shouting in the frozen air

I am wasting my time leaning
from white windows calling out to him
it's no good hoping for more nestling now
his thin cold fumbling fingers
are gloved in great mitts
and flagpoles lie broken
in the shallow snow

the heavy phone clicks
I say *"come down and take away*
my Mister Thomas and his bag
O call him up suddenly
into the City of Words"

The Meditation Look

I am a thin scrap man
I am a torn man from dust city
I am advertising for
a tied-up crosstitch ragwoman
to live in a world of
boxtops and wrappings

      (toy world playhouse play
      dilly dally can you
      won't you learn to lay
      tell me can you learn to play
      the in game out with a shadow?)

I remember how and when I bought
everything I own   I paid down
good money on all the claptrash
that you see   is the empty clock
windless watch going to worry me
now that I have you Dilly Dolly
is it?
Caress is a good word
I paid for it   (all the finer things
      paper angels' wings
      feminine froth and somewhere
      that is somewhere to address
      the grass so green
      and the great obscene
      dahlia heads
      in their nuptial beds)

nod nod your wobble head
I hope you're not straw-stuffed
I hope auntie grace
sewed on your smiling face
and stuffed you with an old
chiffon slip saying *"waste not   want not"*

primmed up her mouth and laughed
like the day she laughed when dinky john
met her at the bus stop with nothing on
but a striped scarf and a tyrolean hat
broken feather in his ear and that
was when she learnt to make patch quilts
and mushroom pickles
how that old stove crackles
in its bed of fieldstones

    auntie from your head
    pluck me a bride for my bed
    one who will live with me here
    far from the mountains
    smiling with a cynic grin
    where your needle has embroidered in
    tears under eyes hard as black buttons

Prospect House

Meatman is sunning on the balcony
Cutting his toenails in full view
Of mothers and sisters sipping tea
In the garden at half-past three
Of a windy dusty afternoon

As I drive back and forth
In my little tin chugger
I admire his physique
Just look at those fine red shoulders
Suffering in the heat of the day
At night he won't sleep some
Sharptooth fly will have
Dug holes above his knees and I
Will worry his dreams

Jack in the Pulpit

The box has a head in it
What else is a box for?
The head is of one of those former queens
I cannot go back to since I made
A commitment to this
Fresh Fields Supervisor

Now look forward to cleaner feet
You bastard of the custard-pie era
"Seriously Jack isn't it time you sunned your
legs on your own balcony?" what ho
For former things? the more you yawn
The more you sleep and

Dream of yourself and a faded lover
Blurred face and name forgotten but
His hands are hot and strong and
Hairy knuckles and white bands
Of bare skin where the golden rings
Have worn through and fallen away

Ergot and After

We were standing on the grass breathing
not even the first word had been spoken
when a great mushroom jumped out of the grass
between us and obscured the trees and the horizon
and the utter blue

Where is your grace O Lord that you
should root my love in such shallow soil
like the bush on the Shield
where every tree falls down
after ten years' growth

"look at that" I said to my love
*"our love is a mushroom as tall as a tower
the towers of drowned cities
were once as tall as this thing between us"*

Come peel the pithy stem
come cut the gray-pink flesh
it is good for us to drink
the juice that trickles from
the torn side of the Lamb
and don't pass up this opportunity
to save Save SAVE
at the great Precambrian post-Christian sale

cry out and say
"we have come to rescue all mushrooms from Campbell's cans"

cream is pouring over them
and I could spray on you
the ultimate in deodorants my mate
why should we smell of mating
when the cry is exterminate
all creepy-crawlies and live
in a grassy Eden alone with you
and detergents to wash the stones of the waterfall
and no more moss

The moss was green and underneath
crept mycelium and worms
twisted together in leafmold
and rotting corpses
now let me rot and nourish your shallow roots
why embalm me when all has fallen to dust
and ashes are in our mouths
let's cut our way into this fungus
and live in a house edible and earthy
or shall we burn up what God saw
when he pushed the C button for the stars
to bubble and burst against his thighs

he knows
you know   I know
what swells in love
what we want is to erupt spray and expand
into a universe

Shall we burn our mushroom to a cloud of smoke?

or shall we dig holes and spawn fungus between the planets?

and between you and me my love
some sort of truce
to prevent murder

No Approach

Look my honey my bird
The walls are painted with words
PEACE NOW
WE WANT NON-VIOLENCE FOR CHRISTMAS

Snow has covered the shacks of our passion
And we are cold saints on the evening shift
Beneath the white I tunnel to you
And stab under the light coverlet
At your cool red center

That's when you fell
With a genuine smile
On your sunset dial
And the doctor pronounced you nearly dead

Twinning

Twinning is what happens somewhere back in far ancestry
And it happens to you my darling
It happens to me
I am bending down to pick the beebleberries
On the flowering tundra when suddenly
A man's behind me behind
And I'm twinning again

They come out of me marching marching two by two
The little men and the little girls
They do me no injury when they come
I swoon away   I don't feel a thing
When I awake I see two small faces
Swathed around with flannel and four eyes
Shifting side to side in the dark

My mother and my grandmother all my aunts have twins
Even my daughter poor ripe Elsie
Is pregnant with them
If only he would not always catch us unawares
Then at least we would know who
Is the father of all these bellyfuls

Visitors' Parking

O Mary Mary lying on the wheel
looking up through rafters
yes you can see through the ceiling
the beams of your eyes dissolve
the joists and the tiles
and though you may writhe and scream
yet calmly you watch the clouds
circling our planet
tears drip from your open eyes
but you are a wax woman
a supple and yellow image
somehow they have managed
to embalm you yelling

kind Doctor Lawson puts his arm round my shoulders
(he is the fatherly type with springing gray hair)
"it's just that she's a broken loony girl"
he says *"the whole damn place is full of them
those are shock treatments we're giving her"*

So then I remembered the day in the woods
when the wheels crunched and crackled
the twigs and the leaves
I remembered the scratch of the branches
along the cartop as we slowly drove away
it was a roofless camp   the trees
grew straight upwards towards the shining sky
as we lay side by side on pine needles

there are two old women with my Mary now
one cackles and the other titters
as they walk her up and down on the mown grass
each holding a hand *"we know her better
than you do dearie"* the fat one says

I peer at Mary through green porthole glass
she is smiling the smile of a clever fish
"in summer" she says *"when all the doors are open*

this place is a madhouse" and then she sits
down on the steps of the white bandstand
hoping the huge brass noise
will drown out the voices
shouting inside her head

"forget it son" says kind old doc benignly
*"get yourself another bit   once the pants
are off them what's the difference?"*

Bertha

Lully my bitch is
Licking strangers' hands these days
I loved her but she wanted
Green shelters and town houses
With air-conditioned stairs
"A *maid arranging irises in*
Tall vases is worth all the words
You pay out George and more"

What she doesn't know is that
I keep my old withered wife
Below stairs ready to take me over
When I get tired of bitty skirt
And big titty

My white wife I haven't looked
At you for years   perhaps
Your watery eyes are still blue
Deep in their baggy sockets

Pay Day

It's that time again
when even our simplicity
must be sustained—I am the sustainer
so in I go
into a tent of webs where I
must pull the rope till the bell tolls
or the threads tangle   here I'll suffer
the tumbling pain of slowly bringing forth
six thousand words of brilliant commentary

my dear there's something of you hard
the pip in the orange
the shell round the egg
are you remembering the arguments
of other evenings or
the snores of other lovers?

your soft pulp is stiffened
until your hand can bear to wind
the threads that tether me

there you stand in the doorway
a round pill of some hypnotic
all that I do is forgotten
as I do it
in the final moment I see you bend
towards me   catch me as I fall
and carry me out for air

Now convalescent arm in arm we pace
slowly along the yellow gravel walks
today is wrapped up and stamped
and sent away but still
tonight remains   Locked in the park
with all the dogs gone home
we sit on the cold concrete side by side
watching the smudgy darkness rise
behind the disappearing gates

II Ribgrass

Granny Looks at the Stars

high above Granny's head
stars are staring and burning
in the slate-blue deep
Granny ties her shawl tighter
around her white ears
and shuts her eyes
and takes off for the great indoors

into the stuffy kitchen
into the tidy house
where everything's strictly folded
everything carefully dusted
(in case she may one day be found dead
she won't leave disorder behind her
for neighbors to tidy up after she's gone)

here Granny sits in her comfortable swivel rocker
licking a dripping Fudgsicle
staring at a sparkling colored
important message from CTV
three young men and a girl
all very lively and hairy are yelling
and twanging against a background
of swaying plastic ribbons and tinsel tassels

Granny looks and licks contentedly
while the tickless clock on the table
soundlessly marks the division of
evening from night   and Timothy
the cat watches the drips on the floor
drip drip from Granny's sweet treat
Timothy watches as though the drips

were drops of blood from a rat
he had killed and was too fastidious to eat

Suddenly a voice out of heaven: *"Turn off the TV Granny*
Put on your second-best
fur coat
Put out the cat"

saith the Lord

"Walk in the yard Granny
Look up at the stars
Give me your honest
opinion
of my handiwork"

saith the Lord

"Why are you piercing holes in me
you wretched nightlights far away"

said Granny lying back in the snow
with her long feet pointing upward
now I know creation is a half-hour drama
I'm watching endlessly
it's a soap opera which never dies
and will always deliver
a daily installment for ever and ever

but she stretched her knotty fingers out
far into darkness until they almost touched
the light bursting from the expanding galaxies

"Damn you God" said the old lady
breathing her last in the frozen potato patch

"All I asked was a Kozy Korner
kitchen cushion cat
chum chew chat
spit spite spat

tell telephone TV
chitter chatter chide
snit snigger snide

What do you mean?
grow groan grain?
green gold gray?
bow be burdened bear?

You have known all along that I don't care
for the fundamental   that I live for the incidental
O Lord stop bugging me do
who am I to call my children's children
out of the plastic playbox
out of charm school
to prance among the stars?"

like the ascending Christ
Granny left her print upon the Earth
not a foot only but broad beam
bowed shoulders and corrugated coiffe
as she fell from the rolling planet
as her small innocent self dived and cavorted
among the heavenly bodies
"Amen" sang the angels

"Amen" said Tim the cat
as he jumped through the bathroom window
and silently sat in her chair

37

Beyond the Alpha Screen

Mildred and my aunt
went on one of those jaunts
over the coral reefs
where you can look through the bottom
of the boat and see the sea turned over
and see the world under water
flitting and killing

"Oh the peace the peace"
cried out my painted aunt
in the broadbrimmed hat

Mildred was timid but she knew
the truth when she saw it
she cut a wide mouth in the glass
with her fingernails

in she dived
into a forest of seaweeds
now she's dancing on the coral apartments
of small polyps
she crushes a spider crab
between her knees

at last there is nothing
left of her but bones
to sink down into the deep
sharks have eaten her up

and all this time my aunt
is taking home movies of the scene
"not everyone" she says
"gets a chance to cruise
in this glorious semi-tropical island paradise"

Videotape

somewhere in Russia
Kakky is dancing
Kakky is dancing in a shiny shift
Kakky is dancing on her bare flat feet
    shaking her belly
    shaking her shirt
    shaking her hair out till it
    breaks and falls
    on her square feet dusty from the floor

a hundred are watching
moving their slow eyes
side to side with her undulations where
  the breasts show in the cleft   where the yellow silk parted
      and where the lips   part
tombstone teeth glimmering between redbrown lips

    all they say is AH   all they do is wonder what the mad life is
        hung somewhere between Greece and Africa
          somewhere between movement and desire
what the drum is
what the dream is   don't tell me this in WESTERN
                  DECADENCE
      Mr. Lecturer
      Mr. Letcher how could he look?
          how could he find time
           to time the beat of her feet
on the splinters?
        stare eyes at the dust from the floorboards
virtues greet all the jerks with horror
what's a life without purpose?
            purpose me only to roll about
           in a bed of love

Saint Katharine come down
come down from the
shaking film Saint Katharine
miraculously moving ikon   girl of the gods   devotee of life
newly nubile   dance
dance round Russia
Kakky till blisters numb your feet

reel over till
the reel over breathing vodka
we   all reel out to the gray street
high over Russia
the wide heavy aircraft slowly roars
full of heavy Soviet Peoples above
and below the clouds
on the plain
on the steppe
highgrass and lowgrass
ridge and cold mountain
they are standing everywhere
staring up at salvation crying

send us only life and breath and fire and Kakky wound in a tin
box

throw it down
on our tower
in our town   let us gather in a hut of corrugated sheets
gather and wonder
worship and revile

O miraculous ribbon unravel the mystery
O let us sit solid
and stolid   and watch Kakky dancing
three times through

caught like a reed
   in the squeeze
   and the freeze of the North night
        where the North Light   is all that is green until
May   and how many
days until then?
      when something might
         spring in
         spring beside the flood from the
           slipping glaciers every day measuring icebergs as they
fall and slowly turn in a dignified dance in the sea
all the long night is illumined
with candles of devotion all the
snow in the boring streets can't
smother the sound of footsteps
in the dark running to the Peopl
es' Palace room 42 where a small
man in a brown jacket will proje
    ct for the eighth time the strong stamp and beat
                    of Kakky's fat feet
         and the sudden and certain jerk of her spine

but the picture fades and film flickers and is broken
the sound whistles
  and wavers and dies
              celluloid stretches and
                 shredded to ribbons
boxes with rusted rims
dumped in the
dump
    after a year or two years or
        ten years who will remember
    Kakky's buckteeth?
    or the kink of her coarse dark hair?

     as the crystal bears the cutting beam
Kakky is dancing in Russia
for there are girls
   glad to be
         wet
         warm and
         willing   they are dancing out of all the houses
and bringing down planes from the skies
      demanding devotion with the strong beat of their hot bare
                                     feet and the slap
of their breasts
on their chests
and the sting of the sweat that runs into their eyes

A Celebration

Our grandmother had gout
(I think it was that)
there were chalk deposits on her knuckles
that stuck right through the skin
she used to amuse us children
by drawing five simultaneous lines
on the blackboard with the back of her hand
it must have been painful

last summer she died

she was drowned in the sea on her birthday
while swimming off Portland Head
it was a cool and windy day
but nothing would keep her
from the stormy water

they buried her on the southdowns
under a hummock of grass

But those limey spikes
grew rapidly in that soil
they branched underground
like the twigs of a great tree
they grew upwards from her desiccating hands

by September they poked out at the surface
a wide circle of little chalky stubs
I think they might have leafed out amongst the short grass
but autumn is a poor time for sprouting

when All Souls' came we lighted
eighty of them for holy candles
they burned brightly for a while
and then they wrinkled and browned
and flickered out

next year they may flower with rockroses
or stiff honeycomb corals

that's one of the reasons
we are waiting and hoping for the spring

Elizabeth Renders

LOEDE   All those times you called me
those four months you phoned me
Every Saturday night at nine
Over the dented land and the crumpled sea
Crying out to me *"Come up to Malmedy
Again"* you said you said you said

ELIZABETH   Is that you my stronghanded
Longlegged brownskinned
Dainty-footed hunter?
Is that the sound of the breath
I know too well I love?
And is that all your answer
(A wheeze and sometimes a cough)

I listen and know you live
Just by the breath ticking
Somewhere in the chest
Yes you are living out there
Far away from my stony hills
And green thickets   You are there
In your hut
In your shack
Awake in the dark

Ask ask ask
Beg beg beg
Please please please
Fly up across the water
Come over to me in Malmedy

ANSWER   Snort shuff   snort shuff
         Gurgle of Alantic
         Click

ELIZABETH   I'm speaking to dead wires
            Sounds shuffling on the airways
            Or transatlantic on the underseas

OPERATOR   If there is no reply madame
           You won't have to pay

ELIZABETH   Not a word
            Not one word

OPERATOR   That will be zero francs
           Zero centimes

ELIZABETH   No not even a word
            Silence

DEITY   Back to the windowseat
        And thoughts of a smug nature
        Partly formed of fear
        Are masking her face
        Evening coming on
        And she was the one
        Always making curly lace
        With her shiny pink fingertips
        How close the net hung down
        How the net tightened
        And folded its fancy web
        All over her as she knotted
        And knotted on   until it covered her
        And wrapped her

Elizabeth Renders is asleep
Waiting for her colored wings
The promise woven into intricate rondels
Of thready linen pressing
Around her and under her until
Its tightness and her weight
Print the roses into her skin
Print a pattern of flowers on her thighs

LOEDE I want to ask when
The child will be freed
When was the cutoff date?
You who are small as the crust of a cocoon
Let me wear your yellowing chrysalid
As an earring then won't I catch the least murmur
As the child stirs in its tiny case?

PHONE Humm humm humm

LOEDE Hello hello
Speak speak
I am ready now
I am ready to listen
Today is my day for answering
Where is the question now
Where is the question?

PHONE Click

The Man from Toledo

The man from Toledo used to sit
every evening drinking
from an ugly square cup

his hands have always been much
older than the rest of him
thick veins stand out on them
a system of blue tunnels
only half submerged
in the papery surface
they used to rest so quietly
one turned upward on his knee
the other bent around
the thick angle of his glass

Did you know that he was once
the boss of an african project?
standing with his hat on his head
and a blueprint clutched
in his hand like a whip
his feet were always placed firmly
a little apart and neither itched
nor moved when the drums beat
only his eyes followed the dark legs
of satiny ladies
as they walked by his window
in the warm dusk

One cold morning
in a white saskatchewan spring
a fiery tongue rested
for a moment on his head
his wife was pleased regarding it
as some sort of happy omen easter hat

the man from Toledo felt the weight of virtue
strutted in his sunday suit and gave
five-minute exhibitions of
speaking with tongues

he insisted on a ministry of healing
there are so many lovely women
suffer from acne and sagging breasts
from fat legs and bloodless lips
his love flowed over milky from the cup
and he decided to lay his hands
on every one of them

last Sunday evening when
the meeting was hushed and thinking of food
and listening to the sound of its own breathing
he suddenly leapt up screaming and dancing and singing
he saw her at last huge figure of Mother Africa
and with her key-white teeth
she bit through his parted lips

a fire was in him
it licked the dome of his satisfaction
it ran in all his arteries
a string of athletes were his corpuscles
his tears dried in the sparkle of his upward gaze

an odor of juices rose up
from her thighs and her grapefruit breasts
swung free out of her cloth
and trapped him into her flesh

he melted into her and became
the skin of her stinging palms
as she clapped and clapped them together

Novella

Early one morning
about seven a.m. mountain standard time
the thin man with the stooping young shoulders and
stick shanks and bony wrists unfolded himself
he stepped out of the fat lady
kop kop on his neat feet
he went down the stairs to the street

now that the thin man climbed out of her
what's left of the fat lady? seven rollers
are stuck to her head
with wads of greasy hair
her doughy flesh is empty
her imposing bosom nothing
but a pair of hollow sweaty falsies
and no legs   nothing but
shiny crumpled skin between
her hem and her husk feet in
their slip slop slippers

what will the milkman say?
no clink and heavy step behind the door
no waiting while she shoves her teeth in while
flustered she wraps a bright blue wrapper
round her great thighs   if she lies
in bed and doesn't answer
and he leaves quarts and quarts
one day soon he will have to call the cops

"Mrs. H don't answer her doorbell
and there are five bottles of milk on her step
I expect she is dead in bed
in her striped flannelette"

"Listen carefully for snores
and distant flushings"

Nothing? Well perhaps tonight the thin man
will come back and climb into the fat lady again
will she know what he's been up to
briskly walking about in the city
selling things door to door
eating at a crumby counter
seeking a fair and easy woman
pinching a thin rump and making a date
and breaking the date
to come running back to the fat lady

Safe at last in this citadel of soft flesh
and the wide face on the pillow smiles
the thin man and the fat lady swing his/her/their strong
legs side to side in the bed kicking
off the covers laughing
under the tumbled quilt

The Holy Fountain

seeing virgins walk
along the banks of a river
who can believe that they will one day be sore?
walking on thin straight legs
bunched together or in single file
wobbling along a sea wall or standing
still on separate posts of a breakwater
as they watch the sea go out
across the empty sound

who can believe that
they will one day be sore?
or slowly plod
heavy with full-term child?

will they arch with desire
and cannot come?

who can believe that at this time of year
seeing men standing
in pissing attitudes
in corners of buildings or by trees
or in the open where the arc is widest
who can believe
that they are so easily buttoned?

did you know that there is an old woman
dressed all in black whose
business it is to defile the altar of Saint Paul?
she is singing about the spider
she is cursing the spider
she is the terrible spider
turning turning and wetting down her legs

now that the well
is boarded up because of the smell
she is the only one who celebrates
the fate of virgins

Night Sermons

Floating with Joan in the dark
following her through gates and doors
which she left a leaf ajar
like a blade slipped between bark and sapwood
following her down saggy steps to her basement
where the cage hangs

She took out a penlight flash
and juggled it around until the light
quivered like a candle flame
and left its strong singeing mark
on the surface of the thick dark

Only in the dim could she believe in him
think of his birdseye heavily closed
under the lid
under the roof of a black cloth
which cylinders—little batteries of her fingers
grasped feeling the dull felted surface
like the hair of a matted deer

when she drew it suddenly away
he fluttered slightly but didn't really
want to move his feet on the perch
let alone fly out
She opened the window   the dark rushed outward
and we could hear the wave
of dithering aspens

She was within her rights to yell
get out get out yellow bird
he had to be thrown over the sill
because he knew of the owl
so did Joan but she found it rather easy
to convince herself of great truths
to the cage to the graceful vault
of my wicker she reasoned
freedom is to be empty

She latched the door of the cage
then pulled the stifling cloth
over her nicely arranged head
sleep sleep she whispered under the flannel
come as an ambush   no one wants to hear
the last cry of a wounded creature

Girl with a Basket

Now comes dusty Beatrice drab girl
With her arms full of bales wound with fresh linen
She lets fall white coils down between long gray fingers
Nor smudges nor smears clear light   cold linen

Beatrice why are you crying as you smooth the sheet
With your dark hand?
She makes a short drain snort in her nose
Being fearful and glad to watch the head cut open
Or green shell belly slit with small sharp knife
Looks down and sees eight rows of seeds
Neatly knitted into a web of pith Her one comfort
The sweet drops that drip from the flesh
Not like tears they run
Like whey from squeezed cheeses

What a Girl Has

When he was a young man
in the German war
my cousin learned a lot
of barrack-room songs

now that he's getting on
he still sings them on Sundays
to the tune of a breathy concertina

> *"If I had what a girl has*
> *If I had what a girl has*
> *I would lie all day at the crossroads*
> *With my legs spread apart"*

No you wouldn't Leon
if you were a girl
you wouldn't do it like that

you would sit in an oaktree
playing softly on your mandolin
with seven colors of ribbon
tied to its stem

you would sit on a branch
and let your bare feet hang down
over the swaying heads
of the endless marching columns
going towards the battlefront

if some of those soldiers
didn't hear your song
did not look up and grasp your dangling feet
and pull you down from the tree
and rape you in the rising dust

then that would be their loss
wouldn't it cousin?

Biting the Hand

Today in the test tube
Tomorrow in the papers

Here's Serafino full of solemn words
"*I knew we should go on*"
(and on and on?)

reflected in his glossy eyes
I see us all rushing Nobelwards
in ships and planes
he's dreaming of prizes now
acclamations for all of us (he's not a selfish man)
and there he stands rubbing clean hands together
squeezing success between his hairy thumbs

but I'm a man needs time
            time to spin out this sharp transparent shell
            and watch the river rise to wet my finger

I saw a thread of hair hang through the keyhole
I pulled and lo a lock hanging through the lock
and then a hank
and then a head of hair

at last a face the infant eyes screwed shut
I thought a shriek would splutter from his mouth
but when he smiled I saw a smiling man
reflecting my green eye in the smoky tube
and when he spoke a god like me said *justice*
and all our feet were kicking at the dust

Serafino is blind

Serafino is deaf

I wish he were dead
squeezed silent in his coffin
helpless between the lights
but he's alive and counting
how many physicists
can dance upon the point of no return

Fragments

A tall man lay down in a hole
And covered himself with earthclods
With the grass side turned inwards
He left his gray helmet on the mound

They took him away and laid him
With the others in their nice neat row
Who was he?

  * * *

We were bending to pick
Wild cyclamen in Normandy
Watching two tethered cows watching us
Longing to trample (bad temper has
Overcome them this afternoon
Because the girl on the bicycle is late)

  * * *

Dead horses from the ditch
Bone against bone
Under the thin grass

My dear child
how small you have grown
how slender the fingers that fiddle
along the fine strings of your hair
and your eyes which used to be
huge sky reflectors have shrunk
to the size of wild green hazels
pushed into your head
behind the drooping lids

> ready to go?
> ready to go
> the deadheads all
> picked off
> the lawn mown
> to the quick
> the washing
> all taken down
> and folded away
> in a basket

the hot bus pants and squawks to a stop
your feet are yellowing birchleaves
skittering down the porch steps

I stretch out my hand
rather rough and scaly
like the claw of an old hen
scratching for a kernel
not even as big as a grain of wheat

you are a winged weedseed
smaller than a flake of dust
a mote that catches in
the driver's eye

III Nettles

It Wasn't a Major Operation

the surgeon joined us
with a long wire he threaded
through your left earhole
and into my right one

when we woke up from the anesthetic
we had to begin practicing at once
every time you nodded your head
I inclined mine
we bobbed together this way and that

when the wire was too taut
there was a knotted feeling in my head
when it was too slack
it looped and caught in my necklace

but now we have got used to
the continual lolling motion
and are able to go
for a short walk every day

this morning while we were
admiring the lilies
a row of birds sat down on our wire

night has fallen now
and they are still here
nine sparrows and a kingbird

Zbigniew

One day my love
your youth ran out of you
as though you were a broken jar
and the ground between us was crossed
by twisting rivulets
drying in the heat
leaving a muddy cursive

my dear I'm sorry
I have to leave you in the house
all afternoon while I
wander in the fields
trying to read the meaning of those marks

come sit in this chair by the window
and watch me

Stefan Sequence

ONE

Because you came on Tuesday
you believed yourself to be
the answer to my disappointment

I did not even know I was wounded
until you made me tell you about it

most days I say to myself
*"I am happy   I can dance
anytime I feel like it"*
these words hang down
from the corners of my mouth

my fingers smell of leaves
and have inky tips

my ears have tent spiders
lolling from them

my feet are always in grass
or in sandals
I could file the rough edges
of my heels if I had time

which are the gray strands
and which the brown?
my body sags at this end of the year
I feel rather tired and abandoned

so come and prescribe me a change of scene
a return to the seashore
it smells of wrack and washed rubber

you all-loving
have you never heard that a coneshell
the most precious of seashells
is the home of a venomous mollusc?

here—catch
I am throwing the thing to you
if you are afraid of its sting
let it fall harmless back into the ocean
saying after me:
>   "*Glory-of-the-Seas*
>   *glory be to you*
>   *and to the shore*
>   *and to the spike grass*"

shall we meet again by chance
or must I make another appointment?

TWO
I want to know
who you are

so while you sleep
I trepan your skull
and creep in
and shut the bone lid
and stick it tight with spittle
here I play the part
of a gallwasp grub
tasting your mind

because of the anesthesia of my teeth
you don't know I am within
destroying you
and digesting you

an old welshman once taught me
to press a bright coin into the earth
of a fresh grave
he said the penny would travel
through the soft soil
and enter into the coffin under the lid crack
and light on the heart of the newly dead
and then his eternal dreams
would be of riches
and travel
and carpeted hotels

you sleep
you sleep
when you are dead
I will press two thorns into your mound
we will be lucky if they light
on your closed eyelids
if they pierce your eyes

THREE
and while the lily floated on the pool
opening itself to the earwigs
and the bees   and to the light
tears in my eyes
I wanted to lily it up
and float on air and water to the skies

and beyond out
where fragments of iron planets fall
but cannot harm the lily or the sun

I wanted bright garden and shade
and not to die as dies the water lily
    snaking it head down
          to the mud
                    you know he has more
                        than a thousand folded petals
                      round his cold core?
                    you know he has more
                        than I know he has

because you have watched him
stretching out his petals
and each one was a hand
they were hands caressing
and hands clutching at each other
          and swords were in some
          lopping off their loves
          because they were old
          or cold
          or looking the other way

            and was the heart an eye?
            wasn't it the heart
            that looked around for enemies and hates
            and wanted to cry out
            and kill
            and come   but eyes have not mouths
            to shout *"a core is not a heart*
            it is the yellow pith part
            from which stamens
      hang upwards smelling strong and sweet"

and thinking *"this is certainly the end of the beginning"*
and begging to be sure
and struggling to pull free
those long roots from the rot
   tell me a good reason
     why I should take the risk
      of discussing who I am
        and who are you
        and which
        is lily
          or mud
            or shining
              air

FOUR

Your skin is translucent
rather than thin china
bumpy and gray in places

your coat is ridiculous
with its contrived holes
and chewed places
somewhere mice
must be using it
for nesting material

probably you are badly fed
your hands are too quiet
if you bent a thin board
it would supply arch
you could not snap it
or crunch gravel with your feet
in heavy workman boots your thin bones
in their soft sheath of little flesh
can hardly carry

we discuss true earthenware
what we will each make in clay

yours is a putty-colored vegetable marrow
with its heavy ribs and striped stem
you will leave out the leaves—
too flat   too soft   too hairy—
you want it all of a piece
under its heavy glaze

mine is a house
small enough to fit into a hand
it has purple onion domes
and a railed balcony
an easter play can be acted on the platform
by a child's five fingers

while we are talking
I think about your feet
which should be out of those boots
at least for a while
because I know them to be that sort of feet
high arched and with thin nails like fingernails

there is no sense in trying to patch your jacket
it should have a whole new nylon shell
to crackle when you walk
and spark in the dry night air
and to coldly let your head slip off
when you fold it for a pillow

FIVE

I am writing to ask you
about your hat
is it knitted straw
or is it soft mail
a silvery mesh?

why did you leave it here
you know I will never wear it
however cold my head is

I dip my finger
my ink is tacky stem juice

write: *glory is what you expected*
write: *memory is an act of mercy*

Untitled

You used to compare
me to a pear
the small end was my head
you said
the thick swelling was myself
under my own apron
that's where the split started
and the flesh parted
down to the ragged core

I say *"look
the core of this fruit is a folded spider"*

I say *"for the first time I have dancing legs"*
and I stretch out all eight of them
trembling towards your hand

you keep your distance
your hat is on your head

you say *"congratulations fractured lady
        I always knew
        I always hoped
        that it would end this way"*

Skeps in the Orchard

We signed the contract

your part was to lie in the orchard
every afternoon and sleep
mine was to sit and watch you
until you wakened

When autumn came
it was rather chilly for both of us
I folded my shoulders into a blanket
as you slept
your breath rose whitely
into the cool air

The shape of your breath is a cone
it is the shape of inside silence
called null
and from the cone's tip
a word is squeezed out
the word is
worm
worm
worm

the word is latent
the word is fishhook

the word has no sound
it has only a shape
O O O

tip of a needle
is a steel cone
it could get broken
into your finger sewing

it could travel up your arm
and about and around you
until it felt your heart's pull
and pierced itself in

your head is a fat cone
wound with heavy brown hair

or

with soft white hair

or

all the hair could fall out
and show your round head
dull newborn mouse pink
and then a word could be written on your head
with the gray cone tip of a lead pencil

the word is grist
                thistle
                brush
                cerise

words are hive bees
each has the shape of its hum
a winged O

they are flying home in a formation
with the shape of a curved blade
returning to the straw hive
with its knotted tip

Nettles

When I am old
I will totter along broken pavements
the strings of my boots undone
smelling a bit strong like any
fat old woman who has forgotten
which day is Tuesday
(my bath night if you like)

stiff my clothes from old dirt
not sweat at my age mumbling
the cracked enamel mug

eleven cats playing
in my weedy yard drinking
my little ration of milk
with me   and withy withy
the cats circle around my house
at night singly filing
in and sleeping on the
saggy stained bed and the chair
and the crumby tabletop

One day they will find me dead
O dead dead
A stinking old bundle of
                              dead

and in my hand
a peeled wand

and in my ear a cricket sitting
telling me stories and predictions

and the time of night

Long Distance

My wife left me
When we were both quite young
She said she was going to visit her cousin
There must have been more to it than that

Last summer she came back
Just before harvest
I awoke and she was there
Baking pies in our wedding dishes

She's a gray and folded woman now
Even her lips are creased
But sometimes when she sits there phoning
A curve of her cheek or arm
Reminds me of the girl she once was

What good is that to me?
I want to remember her always
As she is now

Stopover

Our airport is small and grubby
you have to wait a long time for your luggage

      you say you are in love

if you are in love
why do you pull your hair back like that
why do you tie it so tightly
away from your forehead?

you are taller than I remember
were you not once a small woman
thin and introverted
in a sharp and willful way

and you keep looking into the distance
and you keep saying

      "this must be
      this has to be
      some sort of a beginning"

I break my comb in two
I put the pieces together
back to back
they are the teeth of a face I once knew
black teeth dirty at the roots
reminding me that wild creatures
eat each other
hair and bones and all

lend me a couple of cigarette papers dear
I'm going to play you a song
to welcome you home to the prairies

> *"your lover lies*
> *his tongue is twisted*
> *your lover lies with you*
> *your tongue is twisted too"*

you stare and stare
through the dusty glass walls
while I rub shredded paper from my lips

In the Wilderness

We decided to sleep out on the prairie
zipped naked in one bag
no tent between us and the distant sky

I dreamt we aged quite a bit
our hair grew brittle
our legs got thinner

The wind began to blow

It blew up a gritty storm

We said we ought to get up
and stamp out the fire

The high wind rolled us against a fencepost

A pagewire thorn caught in the skin of my arm

And still we only dreamt the storm and the darkness
nothing could rouse us up out of the grass
until morning when a few flakes of snow
fell on my sleeping hands which were
still gripping the blankets
and the flakes fall and melt on my sleeping hands
each one as it melts staining me
with the tawny stain of speckled age

I cry out in fear
the touch of the snow is like an acid burn

and there you stand in your strength
showing your proud cluster of gray jupiter curls
you dress slowly
you are not even cold in the cold morning
your feet redden in the white grass

I braid my hair

you gently balance a roof of wet twigs
over the ashy fire